Don't Whiz on a 'Lectric Fence

Grandpa's Country Wisdom

Don't Whiz on a 'Lectric Fence

Grandpa's Country Wisdom

GIBBS·SMITH
P
PUBLISHER

Salt Lake City

05 04 03 02   11 10 9 8 7

Published by Gibbs Smith, Publisher
P.O. Box 667
Layton, Utah 84041

Design by Scott Van Kampen

Cover illustration by Ben DeSoto

Printed and bound in the
United States of America

Library of Congress Cataloging-in-Publication Data
English, Roy, 1943-
Don't whiz on a 'lectric fence / Roy English
p.cm.
ISBN 0-87905-755-6
I. Title.
PN6162.E63   1996
818'.5402--dc20   96-5342
                    CIP

The author invites reader response.

Please send any comments to Roy English

1333 Pioneer Parkway East

Arlington, TX 76010

Don't name a pig
you plan to eat.

Early to bed
and early to rise
will pretty much
shut down the
domino game.

Trouble is a
private thing;
don't lend it, and
don't borrow it.

Country fences
need to be horse
high, pig tight,
and bull strong.

The weather can
make a farmer
look mighty smart,
or mighty dumb.

Life is not about
how fast you run,
or how high you
climb, but how
well you bounce.

Keep skunks
and bankers at
a distance.

Don't let the
chickens roost over
the well.

Don't wear
polyester to a
wiener roast.

Life is simpler
when you plow
around the
stumps.

Nothin' on
earth is finer
than a good, slow,
two-inch rain.

16

Mortgaging a
future crop is
saddling a
wobbly colt.

A bumble bee is
faster than a John
Deere tractor.

Don't stand in the trough when you feed the pigs.

Stuff tends to break
when it's loaned or
borrowed.

The trouble
with a milk cow
is that she won't
stay milked.

Always dance
with the one who
brung you, unless
it is your cousin.

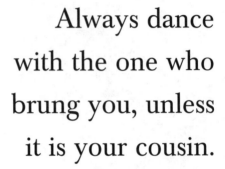

Don't gobble in
the woods during
hunting season.

Don't spread your
blanket where a
cat's been diggin'.

Don't skinny
dip with snappin'
turtles.

The shallower the
stream, the louder
the babble.

Words that soak
into your ears are
whispered, not
yelled.

Meanness don't happen overnight.

To know how country folks are doing, look at their barns, not their houses.

Never lay an angry
hand on a kid or
an animal; it just
ain't helpful.

Country folks
will help a fella
who is down on
his luck, but they
got no patience
with freeloaders.

Hoot owls
and bankers
sleep with one
eye open.

When you're
green, you grow;
when you think
you are ripe,
you get rotten.

The only thing
worse than a
lawn mower that
won't start is
one that will.

Forgive your
enemies. It messes
with their heads.

Goin' to bed mad ain't no fun, but it's better than fightin' all night.

Don't sell your
mule to buy a
plow.

Two can live as
cheap as one if
one don't eat.

No woman is
truly free until
she can change
a flat tire.

Folks don't
change. They just
get more so.

Don't corner
something that's
meaner than you.

 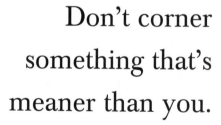

You can catch
more flies with
honey than
vinegar, assuming
you want to
catch flies.

Man is the only
critter who feels
the need to label
the need to label
things as flowers
or weeds.

40

It don't take a
very big man to
carry a grudge.

Don't go hunting
with a fella named
Chug-A-Lug.

You can't unsay
a cruel thing.

Every path has
some puddles.

If it ain't broke,
chances are it
will be.

44

When you wallow
with pigs, expect to
get dirty.

The best sermons
are lived, not
preached.

A fella who is
too quick with an
apology likely
screws up a lot.

Most of the stuff
folks worry about
never happens.

Lazy and
Quarrelsome are
ugly sisters.

There ain't a horse-
hair's difference
between begging
and borrowing.

Stumbling over
the truth can
break a heart.

You can't blame
a worm for not
wanting to go
fishing.

A three-pound
cat can eat a
four-pound fish.

A fella will chase
what runs, and run
from what chases.

Don't sneeze
behind a
skittish mule.

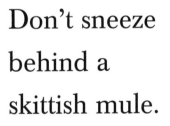

Cow chips need
to dry out for a
spell before you
toss them.

A country dog
never forgets
where he buried
his bone.

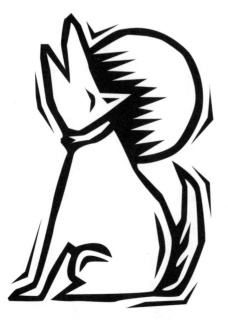

Being neighborly
don't mean stickin'
your nose in some-
body's business.

Nothing is
impossible, except
peeing in a naked
man's pocket.

It's downright annoying to argue with a fella who knows what he's talking about.

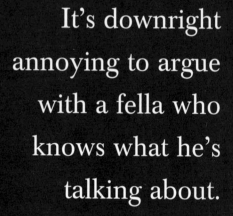

If you run with
hounds, expect
to get fleas.

Coffee is best
when it's saucered
and blowed.

A little tear
absorbs a big pain.

You have to
bust some clods
to make a
crop.

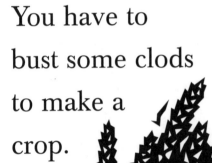

61

Don't ride a new
path at full trot.

An ignorant
fella is hell-bent
on proving his
limitations.

Small minds
and big mouths
have a way of
hooking up.

Debt is like
dragging a
rock in your
cotton sack.

It's hard to keep
a blanket on the
naked truth.

Firewood warms
you twice:
when you cut it,
when you burn it.

A mule can't
help it if his daddy
is a jackass.

72

Some folks are
like ducks; they
seem to glide
along easy
because you
can't see how
hard they work
below the surface.

Country folks
know a lot of
stuff that ain't
wrote down
nowhere.

Country folks
laugh when you
laugh, cry when
you cry, know
when you're sick,
and care when
you die.

If at first you don't succeed, try raising rabbits.

Don't fry frog
legs in an open
skillet.

Don't smoke in
the hayloft.

Interest on debt
never sleeps.

The difference
between young
liars and old
thieves is just a
matter of time.

Hunt every
varmint from
down-wind,
except a polecat.

It's hard to
plant a seedless
grape.

The sweetest
peaches are just
out of reach.

Don't whiz on a 'lectric fence.

For rusty joints,
try a little elbow
grease.

An ounce of
doing is worth a
pound of talk.

Don't rock back
on a three-legged
stool.

A young girl
needs something
to love when
she is too old for
dolls and too
young for boys.
A horse is good.

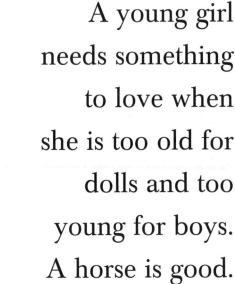

The acorn doesn't fall far from the tree, but some nuts roll a long way from their roots.

You can't bury a
fella just because
he has been dead
for years.

A rooster does
the crowing while
the hen does
the work.

Courtship is
dancing in the
moonlight;
marriage is
washing socks.

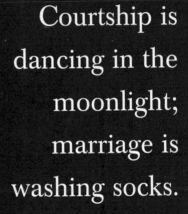

Some folks
have to snore
in self-defense.

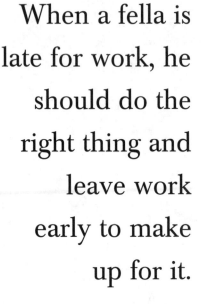

When a fella is
late for work, he
should do the
right thing and
leave work
early to make
up for it.

The world could
use a good worry-
wart remover.

Some city folks
think a square meal
is a sandwich.

The difference
in know-how and
wisdom is in
the doing.

Country folks
can make do with
mighty little.

Divorce changes
the tire; marriage
fixes the flat.

There are lots of
country jobs, but
few positions.

Folks can spot a city fella a country mile away.

Cream rises to the
top, but so does
some other crud.

Turnips and sweet
potatoes will get
you through a
depression. Just
ask Grandpa.

A clinging vine
can choke a body.

 Don't try to hold
a barn cat against
his will.

No jackass ever
got ahead by
kicking up his
heels every night.

Even stubborn
mules know you
have to pull
together.

Some folks have
20 years of
experience;
others have one
year of experience
20 times.

It's easier to
patch a broken
mirror than a
reputation.

The bull is
half the secret
to building a
better herd.

Some fellas have
more wishbone
than backbone.

The only thing
worse than finding
a worm in your
apple is
finding half
a worm.

Don't share a
crosscut saw with
a quitter.

When you feel
neighborly, dust
a little sugar on
your words and
cookies.

A wrinkled brow don't mean a wrinkled heart.

Little pigs make big hogs.

Riddle: What
does it mean
when a country
preacher looks
at his watch?
Answer: It don't
mean nothin'.

A fella can kill
himself with a
fork and spoon.

Whatever the
illness, time is
the best cure.

Feed a cold,
starve a fever,
soak a thorn,
air a wart.

Life is like
juggling pitch-
forks: everyone
knows when
you mess up.

It's best to stop
talking once you've
said all you know.

If wishes were
horses, some folks
would need a lot
of hay.

A fancy title is
about as useful
as the curl in a
pig's tail.

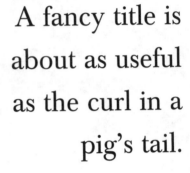

Mount a horse from the left, milk a cow from the right, approach a mule from the front, a billy goat from the rear.

Nothing smells fresher than clean sheets hung in the sunshine.

Advice most
needed is least
heeded.

A cat that licks
his paw may be
scratching his
tongue.

Grave marker
in a country
cemetery–"I told
y'all I was sick."

122

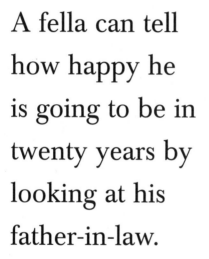

A fella can tell
how happy he
is going to be in
twenty years by
looking at his
father-in-law.

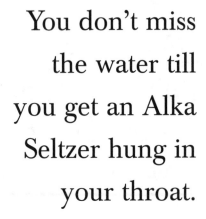

You don't miss the water till you get an Alka Seltzer hung in your throat.

Some folks would
say a lot more if
they didn't talk
so much.

Don't lick a frozen
pump handle.